CHRIST OVER EVERYTHING: LEADING THE YOUTH BACK TO GOD

ANTON C. SEARS

DEDICATION

Dedicated to Anton Sears Jr, Damari Mattice, and David Mattice, my sons. You are the three biggest blessings of my life, and you have been the three most amazing kids a father could ever ask for. You all are going to do great things for Jesus Christ. God has great plans for you to bind to Him.

"I will give you the keys to the kingdom from heaven. Whatever you prohibit on earth will have been prohibited in heaven, and whatever you permit on earth will have been permitted in heaven." Matthew 16:19

CONTENTS

ACKNOWLEDGMENTS

First and foremost, I want to thank my Lord and Savior Jesus Christ. Thank you so much for continuing to knock on my door when it seemed like I would never open it up to let you into my life. Without you, I can't imagine how my life would be right now. You turned my life around when it was at its lowest point. Your love has allowed me to conquer some of my biggest fears in life. Thank you for your grace and mercy that made it possible for me to become an author. Despite all my mistakes and flaws, you still loved and blessed me. Thank you, Jesus Christ; you're my everything.

I thank Tonia, my mother, and George, my father. You both have been the best parents a child could ever ask for. You have sacrificed so much for my brother and me. You have been very supportive and appreciative of all my efforts and initiatives throughout my life. You were always there to support and remind me at my lowest points that I can do all things through Christ. I thank God for the both of you, and I am blessed to have you both. Thank you; I couldn't have done this without you.

I thank Eleanor Watson, my grandmother. You are an amazing woman of God. I'm so glad that God made it possible for us to get back together again. You were always a strong woman. After my grandfather Clarence Watson, the most admirable man I have ever met, left this earth, I saw you grow strong through Christ. Our conversations about Jesus Christ have been priceless. I'm so glad that you encouraged me to write a book for the youth because that was the last confirmation I needed from God to start writing. Thank you.

I thank Geron Sears, my little brother, Uncle Ken, and Aunt Emma. Thank you for all the support and contribution you have extended to me over the years. Christ Over Everything Youth Group is going to do great things for Christ, and thank you for everything you have done.

I thank Pastor Frank Hocker and Minister Barry Hickerson. You two are great men of God, and it was a pleasure learning from you both. I couldn't have had two better examples in my life from whom I could learn the most upright ways to live in Christ and lead my family in the Christian way. Thank you both for the encouragement and advice you have given me; it has played a big part in my life today.

I thank Anthony Gordon, my brother in Christ. Thank you for being a true follower of Jesus Christ. You introduced me to Jesus Christ and showed me the way to him. Your guidance led me to finally open the door of my life to Jesus Christ. Without your help and guidance, none of this could have been possible. I love you brother and may God continue to do good in your life.

Finally, I would like to thank Sharnise, my wife. You are the gift God sent me from heaven. You are truly my backbone, and you always have been on my side. Ever since you came into my life, I have accomplished all that I thought was impossible by me. During my time in school and while I was writing this book, we have not been able to spend much time with each other, and you have been perfectly understanding because you knew that I was fulfilling my purpose in Christ. I don't know how you dealt with my attitude during the time, but you were right there by my side all this while. You complete me. I am whole with God and you in my life. I love you, and there is no way I would have written this book without you.

Special thanks to Janeil Harricharan for formatting this book for print.
http://janeilh.com
.

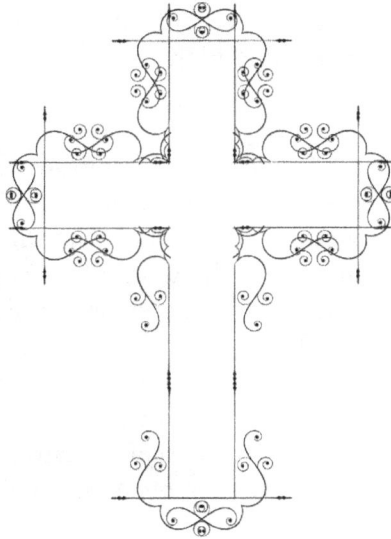

HOW TO OBTAIN SALVATION

Salvation is the forgiveness from God for the sins committed by each and every one of us. It's the gift from God's dear Son Jesus Christ, who paid the ultimate price for the sins of the world. This gift of salvation cannot be earned but should be given by God. The gates of heaven await you when this life on earth is over, and you can reserve your place there by following the steps below:

1. Confess to God that you are a sinner.
"For all have sinned, and come short of the glory of God." (Romans 3:23)

2. Believe in your heart that Jesus Christ is the Savior of the world.
"For God so loved the world, that he gave his only begotten Son, that whosoever believeth in him should not perish, but have everlasting life." (John 3:16).

3. Confess your sins to only Jesus Christ and ask for His forgiveness.

"If we confess our sins, he is faithful and just to forgive us our sins, and to cleanse us from all unrighteousness." (1 John 1:9).

Your Prayer for Salvation

"God, I know that I have not lived my life for You. I realize I have been living for myself, and there is a void in my life that needs to be filled. I so desperately need You in my life right now, and I want You in my life. I recognize the work of Your precious Son Jesus Christ in giving His life for me on the cross at Calvary, and I want to receive the forgiveness that You have granted me through His sacrifice on the cross. Lord, come into my life now, dwell in my heart, and be my King, my Lord, my Savior, and my everything. From this day forward, I will no longer be controlled by sin or the desire to please myself, but I will follow You for the rest of my life. I put my life in Your hands. I ask this in Jesus' mighty name. Amen.

DON'T ALLOW YOUR LIFE TO BE RUINED BY THE SITUATIONS IN LIFE AND THE OBSTACLES IN THE WORLD. THEY ARE ALL TEMPORARY. REMEMBER, LOVE CONQUERS ALL.

CHRIST OVER EVERYTHING—ANTON C. SEARS

ANTON C. SEARS

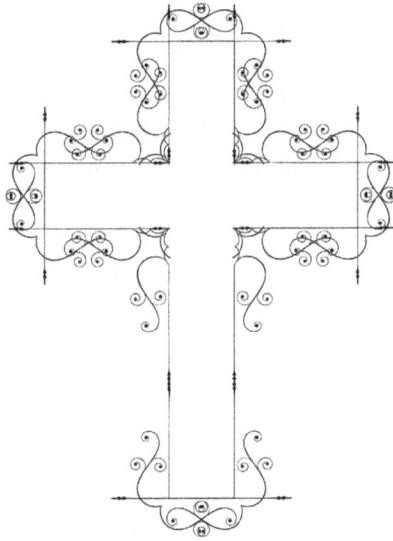

INTRODUCTION: BREAKING THE ICE

There's fun, failure, and then there's redemption. I have no regrets about the situations that occurred in my life that led me to Jesus Christ. I see so many adolescents falling victim to the ways of the world, rejecting the ways of the God as I once did. Knowing that there is a better way to live, I feel it is only right to tell my story as a living testimony to how God changed my life.

Greg Laurie, the American author and pastor, once said about personal testimony is that "One of the best ways to "build a bridge" with a person who does not have a relationship with Christ is through your personal testimony."

It is a lot of people in this world who badly need the presence of God in their lives. There is no sense in gathering information and gaining knowledge if you do not share it with others. Allow me to break the ice by providing a testimony of how I became a follower of Jesus Christ.

When I was a kid, I believed that there was a God who created the universe and everything in it. I believed that when people died, they either went to heaven or hell. I was sure about the requirements to go to heaven, and I thought if you didn't kill anybody you qualified to go to heaven. I didn't grow up in a house where we went to church each and every Sunday. My family and I attended church randomly, the visits mostly being on holidays. My grandmother had a small Holy Bible on her bookshelf, and she used to read it occasionally. I remember walking around softly in the house at night trying not to disturb her. Despite growing from a kid to an adult, my logic and ideas about God never changed. I even talked to him and asked for the things I wanted in life, such as a new car, job, or girlfriend. But believing that there is a God and knowing that there is a God are two totally different things. I believed that He existed just like everybody else did. I failed to find out for myself by searching for the facts of his existence. When something is created, the creator and the creation shares a relationship like that of a father and son. God and I did not have a relationship; it was more like I rubbing a genie bottle for wishes to be granted. The creator also gives his creation instructions for guidance and how to operate according to the purpose it was created for. God blessed me with life every morning, a great job, good health, food, and shelter—the little things people take granted for in life.

It was a Tuesday night, November 24, 2009, to be exact. I was 27 years old then. I had gone out with a couple of friends to a bar. After having much fun and consuming a lot of alcoholic drinks, I called it quits for the night and started to drive back home. Driving down the road on Eastlake, Ohio, I was driving at over 40 mph in a 25-mph speed limit road. After a couple of minutes on the road, all I could see were flashing blue and red lights. I was quickly pulled over by the Eastlake police. A policeman walked over to the driver side window and said he pulled me over for swerving from lane to lane. I also felt that he smelled the liquor on my breath, as I talked to him while sitting in my car when I gave him my driver's license and car insurance. The policeman asked me to step out the car and perform a field sobriety test to see if I was drunk or not. I had seen field sobriety tests happen all the time on television. I thought to myself how could I fail. I knew I wasn't swerving from lane to lane. I knew I wasn't drunk and passing this test would be a piece of cake. The policeman asked me to walk in a straight line. The first three steps went great; after the third step, my whole body shifted to the left and fell on the ground. As I got up from the ground dusting myself off, I started pleading to the policeman for another chance, blaming my failure on slipping on a rock. He declined, and he quickly took me to the backseat of the police car and sent me off to jail. Sitting in the corner of the backseat of the police car I couldn't believe this was happening, as I had never been in this kind of trouble my whole life. I reached Eastlake city jail around 2 am in the morning afraid to call my mother because I knew I had dropped the ball big time and who wants to tell their mom "Hey, Mom. I am in jail. Can you come and bail me out?" It felt so odd being in jail—not because I felt I was too good to be in jail, but because I worked at a correctional facility. I used to go out partying and get drunk every weekend. Every time I got pulled over by the police, I just showed them my correctional officer badge, and they let me go. I guess there wasn't any more chances for me to get out of jail. Quite contrary to the usual, I was the one being put in jail instead of me putting somebody in jail. I sat down on the thin mat on the cold floor. I heard the steel gate of my cell closing, and then I got up and ran to the cell gate to get the officer's attention. I was charged with a Driving under the Influence (DUI). I didn't know how long I was going to be in jail. At that moment, my whole life flashed before my eyes. Confined in the jail cell, I fell asleep as the effects of alcohol and partying took a toll on me. When I woke up hours later still feeling the effects of the alcohol I consumed, all of it felt a bad dream, and I asked myself how all of this could happen. The kid I once was and now the adult I am believed that there was a God, but I did not include God in my life. Money, women, cars, and popularity had driven me in life so far. Being confined in the cold cell made me so upset and embarrassed that I even contemplated killing myself. Being a correctional officer, I knew that the officers made rounds every half an hour if not later, so I knew drowning myself in the toilet would have been a success. The water-level in the toilet was too low, and my head hurt too much even to think of another way to kill myself. It wasn't only the embarrassment that I led me to contemplate committing suicide, but I couldn't think of any reasons to live anymore. Later, I woke up sober from a nap. Then I came to the realization that I had almost made the worst decision of my life. My mind wasn't clear at all; I also realized that I needed help to live better. I was grateful that I didn't get into an accident on the road, probably hurting or killing myself or someone else. I didn't want to contemplate suicide ever again. My mother and father arrived at the Eastlake jail the next afternoon as they had somehow found out my whereabouts, and I was released on a personal bond, which the officer gave me because it was my first time getting in trouble.

Before the incident, I used to think I was a good person, as I wasn't out in the world stealing or killing or physically harming anyone. All I used to do was drink a lot to the point that I couldn't go on without it. I used women for my satisfaction and partied hard every chance I got. It was my way. How could I ever think I was a good person despite committing acts that got me sent to jail? If I was breaking the laws made by human beings, I couldn't imagine how many of God's laws I had broken. Before the incident, I thought that if I died, I would go to heaven, but little did I know I was hell-bound.

The day after I was released from jail, it was Thanksgiving holiday, November 25, 2009, to be exact. I went to work still feeling terrible. I had a co-worker called Anthony Gordon who always used to tell me about Jesus Christ. I never wanted to hear what he had to say until the day I had hit rock bottom. I spoke to Anthony that night at work. He didn't laugh at me or reprimand me. Instead, he told me how God had changed his life through his Son Jesus Christ. After the conversation, he presented me the Holy Bible. After the days at work and being on the phone with him, I engaged myself in reading it more and more each day. I even found myself ignoring my friends and sidelining having fun and playing video games just to read, as it became more and more interesting.

The night before I gave my life to Jesus Christ, I was reading a book by Bill Wiese called *23 Minutes in Hell*. As I reached the chapter five of the book, it contained short stories about people giving their life to Christ after they read the book 23 Minutes in Hell. One of the stories, in particular, caught my eye. A teenager had given his life to Christ, and as he got older, his life became troublesome. As an adult, he got involved in drugs and alcohol, frequenting jails and hospitals. After stumbling across a CD based on Mr.Wiese's book, he recited the prayer of salvation provided at the end of the CD. Then, he called his mother to tell her how his life had changed and wanted to go to church with her the following Sunday. He died in his sleep that night.

After reading the sad story, I began to cry. Being already convinced of what I was reading in the Holy Bible, I didn't want to go another day without being on the right terms with God, whom I truly knew existed for myself and not based what other people believed. On February 22, 2011, I repented for my sins and accepted Jesus Christ as my Lord and Savior. I freely made the choice to give my life to Christ and follow Him. The words contained in the Holy Bible was like that in no other book I had ever read. The words were so unique that it had to come from God because no man or woman could have ever had obtained such knowledge. It gave me clear answers to how and why there is so much evil in the world and why it's ruined because of the sins of humanity.

The Holy Bible states, in Genesis 1:31, that "Then God looked over all he had made, and he saw that it was very good!" All the humans and animals in the world were good and free of violence and evil; so, what led the world to become such a disaster? In the Book of Genesis, Chapter 2, it is stated that Adam was the first human being to be created by God. Adam was free in the garden of Eden, with the job to look after it. He had access to any tree in the garden except the tree of knowledge of good and evil, which he couldn't eat from. Eve, Adam's wife, was created after him. Eve, just like Adam, was responsible for the garden, so she knew about the tree of good and evil. Genesis 3:6 states that

"The woman (Eve) was convinced. She saw that the tree was beautiful, and its fruit looked delicious, and she wanted the wisdom it would give her. So, she took some of the fruit and ate it. Then she gave some to her husband, who was with her, and he ate it, too."

Satan, in the form of a snake, convinced Eve to eat from the tree of good and evil. She gave Adam some of the fruit right after she had eaten. Satan is the ultimate nemesis of God and those who follow Christ. Satan did not make Adam and Eve disobey God; they made the choice to do so on their own. Similarly, Satan had no effect on me drinking and using women for my satisfaction, as I made the choice to. God gives us, as his creation, the free will or free choice to make our own decisions in life. God loves us so much that He did not program us all as robots to love and honor Him the way He wants. If God did so, it wouldn't be an act of love, as it has been forced upon us. God wants us to go to him on own accord. With that being said, we made it possible for evil to exist in the world today. McDowell & McDowell (2012) states that "Evil came from an abuse of a good power called free will."

Satan sets the stage, but he doesn't make us do anything; he just influences our thoughts, actions, and attitudes. From that day Adam and Eve disobeyed God, sin entered the world and ruined God's perfect world. Sin can be defined as the wrongdoing that violates God's will. As we continue to sin and disobey God, the world continues to get worse, and Satan, being the mastermind behind all evil, influences everything we see in the world. I see that the youth today desperately needs a better outlook on life and needs God in their lives Throughout the book, I will be exploring the areas in life that have been misleading the youth away from the ways of God. My goal is to steer the youth to the glorious light of Christ to live the life God intended you to live and out of the darkness away from Satan. LET`S TALK ABOUT IT.

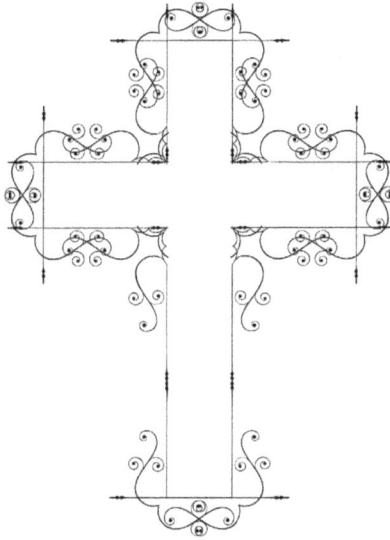

CHAPTER 1: IDENTITY THEFT

"Define yourself radically as one beloved by God; God`s love for you and his choice of you constitute your worth. Accept that, and let it become the most important thing in your life."

—Brennan Manning

Nothing is worse than someone stealing your identity. Identity theft is one of the most active crimes in the world today. When an identity theft takes place, a person's life is taken over by another by stealing that person's credit cards, email accounts, social media accounts, social security numbers, utility bills, and bank statements. Imagine someone has taken over your life without you even knowing it. By acquiring all your information, infiltrating your credit report and credit history, there is no limit to what a criminal can do with your personal information. Practically, when it comes to identity theft, the victim gets used for someone else's benefits in life. Identity theft puts the victim in a situation of having to prove who they are to a greater extent than what the criminal had to do to steal their identity in order to regain their life back. The crime of identity theft can be said to be happening in the lives of youth today. The youth have lost their identity, living their life through someone else instead of themselves. However, in this case, contacting Trans Union, Equifax, or Experian will not help at all.

All of the humanity has become the victims of identity theft, separating everyone from its rightful source of identification—God. It isn't that humanity chose to lose sight of their true identity, but the choice Adam and Eve made to eat from the tree of good and evil brought sin into the world, distancing the relationship man had with God because of Sin.

"It's your sins that have cut you off from God. Because of your sins, he has turned away and will not listen anymore." (Isa 59:2)

Satan has altered the relationship between God and the youth, causing you to lose your identity to use you for his gains. Just as he stole your identity, your identity can be recovered by being reunited with God through Jesus Christ. The way you perceive yourself is what forms your core views in life. In life, you're either living for Satan or living for Christ; there is no grey area in between. Everyone has a worldly identity and a spiritual identity (1 John 3:10). As the world is no longer perfect, and humanity is now sinful, the youth tend to get drawn to the wrong people and other idols, failing to look up to God for guidance. Sin is very amusing—it promises fun, excitement, and pleasure. The new philosophy of the world today—YOLO (You Only Live Once)—has adolescents indulging in sin without the afterthought that there is a spiritual life after this life on earth. The youth in the world is growing up without any biblical guidance from parents or any adult supervision. It is misleading them and make them feel like the world validates them for who they are, the way they act, and pose to be. The youth is the future of the world. Satan knows that if he can control the youth, he can control the future. Satan wants to control the youth and lead them all to hell. Satan targets the youth because they are more vulnerable to his deceptions. Satan influences you and steals your identity, as he has for years. It's time to take your identity back with Christ.

God Wants You Back

You are so special to God that He only made one of you so purely and uniquely. You were created in his image (Gen 1:26). Being created in God's image doesn't actually mean you are a little God, but it does mean that we have the ability to demonstrate his personality and character in the world. You have the ability to love others, and love is what the world desperately needs. You are capable of compassion and enjoying life with a solid relationship with God. You discover your true identity the more you draw yourself to God.

Ortberg (2014) states that "When my soul is not centered in God, I define myself by my accomplishments, or my physical appearance, or my title, or my important friends. When I lose these, I lose my identity."

You might have been called some harsh names in the journey of life such as ugly, fat, stupid, or something even profane, and they probably hurt you, but words from others shouldn't define who you are. That's up to God. According to God, you're fearfully and wonderfully made (Ps 139:14); he calls you the "Apple of His Eye," meaning you're precious to God and that He adores you.

The opinions people hold of you don't define who you are; they don't validate you. Your identity is not determined by what you have achieved in life—the things you have done right or the things you have done wrong. How you identify yourself determines your way of life. If you are what only you achieve in life, you will find yourself doing the most to find happiness within yourself. If you listen to what God says about who you really are and embrace His identity in you, you will find freedom in Jesus Christ and live out the plans He has for your life. You are God's creation, and when you start to see yourself the way God sees you, you will be able to walk in confidence because you trust the one who answers the question, "who am I," and that is God.

Prayer

Dear heavenly Father, I am thankful for all You have done for me. I'm thankful for You not allowing me to die in my sins and giving Your Son Jesus Christ as a ransom for me. I confess my sins to You Father and ask for Your forgiveness. I have made wrong choices in my life that led me to worship idols and allowed others to validate my identity. Lord, please give me a new vision to not only realize who I am in Christ but also to look at others who have hurt me in life over the years and lead them to You as well. Thank you for giving me a new insight into life and a new identity. Lord, I praise You for your everlasting love and leading me out of bondage. In Jesus' name, I pray. Amen.

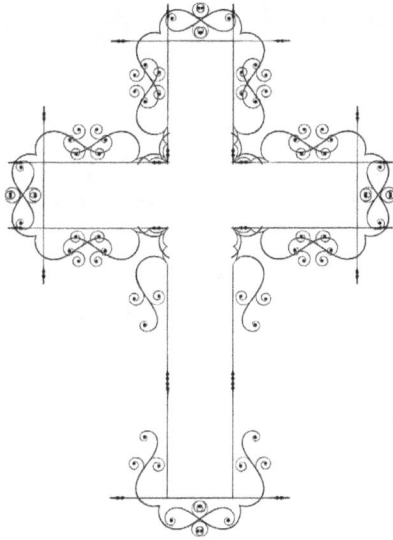

CHAPTER 2: PURPOSE IS FOUND ONLY IN GOD

"But I have spared you for a purpose—to show you my power and to spread my fame throughout the earth."

—Exodus 9:16

Everyone born into this world has a purpose in life. A life with no purpose equals to a meaningless life. Finding the reason why you were created isn't something you do on your own. Your purpose is not based on your childhood dreams or career choices. To answer the question, "What is my purpose in life?" requires answering other questions first such as "How do I find out my own purpose in life?" "How do I figure out what my purpose is?" "Can someone else find my purpose in life for me?"

Thinking about finding life's purpose reminds me one of my favorite quotes from the movie *The Matrix Reloaded*. If you have seen the movie, you will know that the villain in the movie is Agent Smith, and he talks about purpose. In the playground scene involving him and Neo, he states, "There is no denying reason, no denying purpose, for as we both know, without purpose, we would not exist. It is purpose that created us, purpose that connects, purpose that pulls us, that guides us, that drives us; it is purpose that defines, purpose that binds us."

The quote from the movie relates so much to humanity finding their purpose in life. Many teenagers and young adults in the world hold the view that they have no purpose in life. So, they live life by any means. Such a point of view values life so less that it is not a serious matter when they go to jail or take someone else's life. God created us all with a purpose in life, and the only way to find it is to rebuild a relationship with Him through Jesus Christ. God's purpose for all of you is to draw yourself to him, connect yourself to him, guide you daily, bind you to him, and, most of all, it will drive you when life seems meaningless. If you don`t allow yourself to find purpose in God, you will allow something else, such as money, lust, pride, fear, or the expectations of others, to take over.

Your purpose in life is to praise God
"He alone is your God, the only one who is worthy of your praise, the one who has done these mighty miracles that you have seen with your own eyes."
(Deuteronomy 10:21)

In life, we take the little things for granted, such as waking up in the morning. We wake up every morning already upset. Perhaps it's because of something that happened at work, school, or events that didn't go your way. You don't realize that God has granted you another day to enjoy life because you don't have the power to wake yourself up. Therefore, God should be praised each and every day. We tend to praise the wrong things in life. Think about when you watch your favorite athletes on TV. They score, and you praise them. When your favorite artist performs their hit song, you praise them. It's nice to be happy about others' accomplishments, but the one who created them and gave them such talents and gifts should be praised, and that is none other than God. God is behind everything we have in our lives. He deserves praise.

Your purpose is to worship God and him only.
"For God is Spirit, so those who worship him must worship in spirit and in truth"
(John 4:24)

Worship is getting out of yourself for the love of another person. Worship is a lifestyle and not something you occasionally do. Just like you can praise the wrong person, you can worship wrong things as well. Wrong worship follows the guidelines of money, Satan, idols, power, and possessions. The act of worshipping anything or anyone other than God can lead to a life separated from him.

Matthew states, "No one can serve two masters. For you will hate one and love the other, you will be devoted to one and despise the other." (Matt 6:24).

Materialistic things and people should not consume you to the point of taking over your thoughts, time, and efforts that God deserves. True worship of God is not forced but comes easily as you live your life for him. God tests us; God challenges us; God saves us; God provides for us; God protects us; God gives us gifts. He does all of these because He loves us. God wants to be part of your life, and, in return, He wants your praises to be to Him; He wants you to worship Him and Him only; He wants you to love Him, and, most of all, He wants you to find your true purpose in life.

Prayer

Dear heavenly Father, thank You for giving me a purpose in life. I'm very grateful that despite all the wrongs I have committed in my life, You still have a purpose for me. I can now experience the joy of abiding in You to bring a new life to others through Jesus Christ. I realize that throughout my life I have praised and worshipped the wrong things, and now I know You deserve it all. Father, help me keep a positive attitude when things do not go well in my life and increase my confidence in You so that I will hear You when You speak to my heart, knowing that You're with me to fulfill the purpose You have set for me. I thank You and love You. I give You all praise, glory, and honor. In Jesus' name, I pray. Amen.

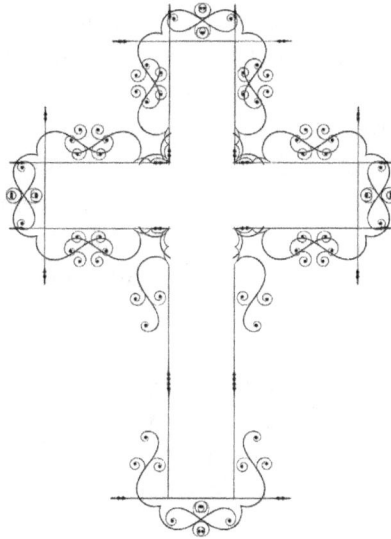

CHAPTER 3: SEXUAL IMMORALITY/CELIBACY

"Run from sexual sin! No other sin so clearly affects the body as this one does. For sexual immorality is a sin against your own body."

—1 Corinthians 6:18

From early on in our lives, we are taught about sexual intercourse and how babies are made through the story of the birds and the bees by our parents or other adults. Frankly, I wasn't a huge fan of the story since my mother explained it to me the first time while waiting for food at a restaurant. From middle school to high school sex education classes are offered to students to make them aware of the dangers of sex. The human body experiences changes in it as the body produces hormones in the teenage years of our life. Hormones help in physical growth and bring about sexual development throughout the teenage years and until the adult stage in your life. They also influence your moods, emotions, and sexual feelings, and they become stronger. As the hormones take their course, puberty hits, transforming your childlike body to an adultlike body for sexual reproduction. Once the hormones and puberty take their course, the attraction to the opposite sex becomes more intense. The attraction towards the opposite sex is normal whether you are attracted to the person's physical appearance, status, or personality. Sexuality plays a strong part in the world today. If you're not having sex in today's world, then it is considered that something is wrong with you. The media, mostly on the TV and in the movies, portrays the human relationship to be nonexistent without sex being involved. Music also promotes sex and paints a picture in our minds that cause us to relish our sexual desires. So, with all these influences in the world, it's easy to find yourself becoming sex-crazed and looking for someone to satisfy your sexual appetite.

Nonetheless, sexuality is God's design, and He reserved the gift of sex only in a marriage. He sets the standards. Marriage has come to be deemed a redundant idea in society and is no longer considered normal or valued, as the "I can do what I feel like" attitude has taken over our minds. Anything outside God's guideline of the gift of sex is a misuse, and if it's being misused in a way that does not glorify God, it becomes a sin. Hence, the gift of sex becomes sexual immorality— sexual activity outside of the bounds of biblical marriage. The following are some examples of sexual immorality:

- **Fornication:** The sexual intercourse outside of marriage.
- **Adultery:** The voluntary sexual intercourse between someone who is married and someone who is not their spouse.
- **Homosexuality:** The sexual attraction to someone of the same sex.
- **Prostitution:** The occupation of engaging in sexual activity with someone for money.
- **Bestiality:** The sexual activity between a human and an animal.
- **Masturbation:** The stimulation of one's genitals for sexual arousement usually with one's hand.
- **Pornography:** Sexual videos, writings, and pictures that generate sexual arousement.
- **Incest:** Engaging in sexual intercourse within the family.
- **Lust:** A strong sexual desire for someone

The above examples are all outside of God's design of sex. Everything God has made is good (Gen 1:31), including sexuality. The world has come to consider sexuality as a personal right, allowing them to do as they please. Our sexual disobedience has created many maladies in the world such as perversion, child molestation, sex addiction, abortion, to name a few. God has set standards for our own good so that the gift of sex will be enjoyed to have pleasure as it was designed for. Sins come with their fair share of consequences. When sex is used outside God`s design, we're not just hurting ourselves but others as well. The rise of abortion, adultery, rape, divorce, pornography, and the number of kids growing up without the company of their both their parents can be attributed to the abuse of God`s gift of sex. Above all, sexual immorality breaks the relationship you have with God. If we fail to recognize God`s standards, we will fall victims to our lust, and it will dictate all our decisions regarding sex. Sexual immorality should be avoided; you should control your body so that it is righteous and honorable to God and not lost in passionate lust.

The following are some tips to avoid sexual immorality:

1. The battle of sexual immorality starts in mind. Educate yourself to know what God says about sex. Satan knows your weaknesses and will use them to lure you into disobedient, as he did with Eve in the garden of Eden (Genesis 3:6). Be careful about where you let your mind wander off. Imagination is the starting point of sin.
2. Pray Often. Depend on and communicate with God and rely on the Holy Spirit to accompany you when temptation comes your way and help strengthen you in the fight against Satan.
3. Do not put yourself in a position where you can be easily tempted. Remember, Satan only sets the stage; he doesn`t make you do anything.
4. Talk to others about sex (Accountability). This fight cannot be won alone. You need help from God and other true professing Christians. Find others you can trust and be open about your struggles.
5. Remember the cross. Jesus Christ died for all our sins, including sexual sins. Remember no one is perfect in the

world.

6. Forgiveness from Christ is available. If you fall into a sexual sin, you can be forgiven. So, repent, ask for forgiveness, and live for God.

Sex is a beautiful thing, and indulgence in it should be reserved only for marriage. So, don't cheapen your experience; you're worth the wait.

Prayer

Dear heavenly Father, I am very thankful for Your grace and mercy. I understand now that sex is a gift from You and only reserved for marriage. Going forward Father, I ask for Your guidance so that I will not fall into the temptations of lust. Lord, You know how easy it is for me to stumble, but when I fall, You are there to pick me up. Father, when the times of temptation come, help me to remember to fall down and kneel and pray and seek You. Thank You, Father, for helping me be victorious over sexual immorality. I give You all praise, glory, and honor. In Jesus' name, I pray. Amen.

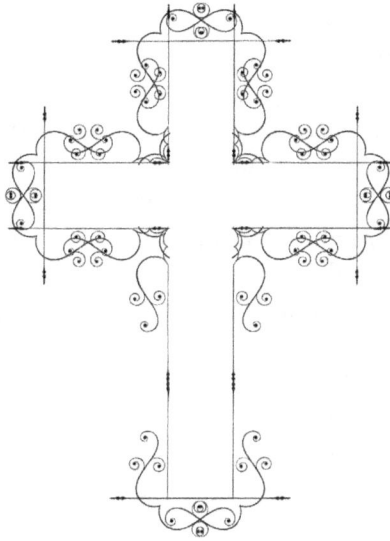

CHAPTER 4: CELIBACY/KNOW YOUR WORTH

"God puts so much value on you, you need not care about opinions, thoughts and words of others."

—Anton C. Sears

"Lord, please forgive me. I will not do it again," were the first words of my prayer on the Christmas morning in 2011. The previous night I had attended a family Christmas party. It was nice to see my family on Christmas Eve, and reminiscing about old times and joking around couldn't have gotten any better than that. By then, I had been a devoted follower of Christ for ten months, starting from February. I didn't drink alcoholic beverages anymore; I didn't smoke anymore, and I had made a vow to myself and God that I wouldn't have sex until I got married. Hours into the party, alcoholic beverages began to be served. My initial thought was to leave, but I felt I was strong enough to be around them. I thought that if others offered me any drinks, I would just refuse them. After several offers, I gave in very easily, as my resolve had broken and consumed three drinks. As I was not in my right state of mind, I didn't listen to my conscience and ignored it and kept on going reverting to shades of my former self. I was tempted to do the wrong thing, and I knew it and couldn't stop myself. I asked myself what's the worst thing that could happen. I reasoned that I would just stay the night over at my family house and not risk going back to jail again. The drinking led me to call a female friend of mine I hadn't seen in years, who had just come to Cleveland to visit her family. Later that night, we met at my apartment and had sex. The next morning, I woke up clear minded with the alcohol out of my system. It seemed like God was staring down at me, upset. I began to start crying ashamed of how easily I had gotten off track, and I told God the exact words that I will not have sex again until I'm married.

Practicing Abstinence

Practicing abstinence isn't as simple as a walk in the park, especially since it involves trying to restrain yourself from sinning. But a celibate life is very fulfilling, as it allows you to discover your self-worth and allows you to be spiritually closer to Christ. Embrace your singledom until God sends that special person your way, or you can continue to give all your time to the God. Don't risk wasting your virginity because it's the homecoming dance or prom or because others are telling you it's the cool thing to do and everybody else is doing it. You should respect yourself and refrain from such indulgence.

So, why should you save sex for marriage? First, sex outside of marriage damages one physically. There is no such thing as "safe sex" when sex is misused. Negative effects come into play, creating more negative effects in our lives. Abortion, AIDS and other sexually transmitted diseases, unwanted and unplanned parenthood are just a few of the consequences. If a child is born, the actions you take will affect the child's life, along with your partner's life and your family. As there is no commitment between the sexual partners, any one of you could run from the responsibility, resulting in single parenting or the child being abandoned in an orphanage. You should save sex for marriage because it can damage or even break the relationships between people. Sin always separates you from God. Your failure to follow His commands not to have sex before marriage shows a lack of self-control on your part and displeases Him. Moreover, if people who know I am a follower of Christ come to know that I am sleeping with women other than my wife and teaching the word of God at the same time, I will be labeled as a hypocrite, giving Christ a bad name. People will not respect or trust me; I would be giving Christ a bad name, and, most of all, I would be disobeying God.

If a man and a woman truly love each other and want to be sexually intimate, they should marry as God has advised. If two people can't wait until marriage to have sex, how can they trust each other to be faithful in the marriage? Willing to make a covenant with each other and to form a solid foundation under God is worth the wait. If you have already disobeyed God's command to abstain until marriage for sex, it's not too late to make a change. You may ask yourself, "How can I become a virgin again if I already had sex?" The apostle Paul stated that "Therefore, if anyone is in Christ, the new creation has come: The old has gone, the new is here!" (2 Cor 5:17)

That means that you are now a new creature, and your past is old news. As human beings, we sin daily. However, as Jesus Christ died for the sins of humanity, we can go to Him because He is faithful and forgive us if we ask for forgiveness for our sins (1 John 4:8). In life, you might have been victimized by others, but this time you are nobody's floor mat to be walked on. You are the common denominator in any scenario or situation you set foot in your life. You're amazing; you're unique; you're worth it, and, most of all, you are a child of God.

Continuing with my story, I gave my life to Christ, and I still fell short of his glory. Before the vow, I made to God to not fornicate again until I was married, Satan didn't go easy on me either. I dealt with temptations from all over—from the temptations to watch pornography to that to sleep with my female friends. I turned down all the offers and opportunities thinking about how hurt and awful I felt on Christmas Eve. I came to the conclusion that if God wanted me to be with a woman, He would send her my way. I decided it was time to stop chasing women in the hope of finding the right match, and it was time to get closer to God. I didn't care if I was single the rest of my life; I was worth more than that, and it was time to start acting like a true follower of Jesus Christ. Everybody is a Christian nowadays, but nobody lives like it. In this world, if you take care of your character, your reputation will take care of itself. I kept my head in the Holy Bible and lived the word of God, and that helped me to not fall into the trap of fornication. Finally, on April 13, 2013, I went on a blind date. I had never done something of the sort earlier, and honestly, I didn't care too much for it. Who would've known that the woman I met that day would end up being my wife one day? Her name was Sharnise. One day, Sharnise and I went out to eat at a bar and grill called Scorchers. We were going steady for about two months then. She told me that she doesn't see us waiting to have sex until we were married. I replied, "Well, I don't see us being together because I'm not about to disappoint God again." She realized I was serious about waiting to get married to have sex. Sharnise and I got married on November 10, 2013, and are currently married. We didn't get married quickly because we wanted to have sex, as I always followed a dating guideline. It takes thirty days to know if you want to start a relationship with somebody and sixty days to know if you want to spend the rest of your life with that person. I wanted to be with the woman God gave me soon as possible. The moral of the story is as follows: In life, we don't want to wait for the things God has lined up for us. We attempt to do things ourselves, thinking we know what's best for us, and wrong things end up happening to us in our lives. When I finally gave God all my attention, He blessed me with the things I longed for. Believe, what God has done for me, He will do for you also.

Prayer

Dear heavenly Father, I thank You for Your gift of celibacy so that I can devote all my time to You. When I got tempted to have sex, You offered the gift of marriage so that I will not violate Your commandments. Father, please show me a way out when I am tempted to have sex and falling victim to the temptations Satan throws my way through the Holy Spirit. How awesome it is that when I fall short, I can repent and ask for forgiveness through the work Jesus Christ has done on the cross destroying sin. For the rest of my life, I pray to live a life not in sexual immorality but in singleness until You honor me with a spouse who loves You. I thank You and love You, and I pray for all things in Jesus' Name. Amen.

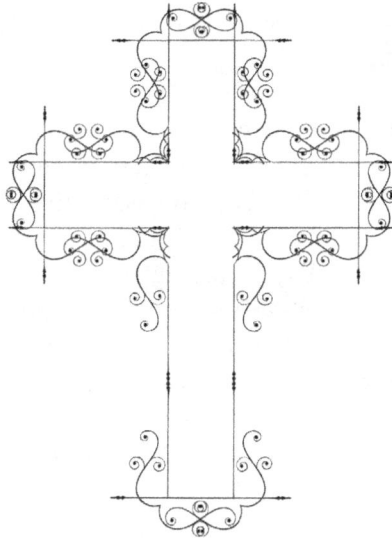

CHAPTER 5: DON'T LET DEPRESSION DEFEAT YOU

"Depression is a serious condition. When we fall into it, we are no longer the one controlling our thoughts, but our thoughts control us."

—Anton C. Sears

Wouldn't life be so much easier if we didn't have to wrestle with depression? The problems we face in life would be so much more manageable if they never existed. Depression is usually triggered by the situations and problems in life that we bring upon ourselves. Depression is a state of mind rather than a sin, which affects us. Honestly, who hasn't been down emotionally and physically in life? When we are emotionally and physically drained, the thoughts that occur in our minds suck the life out of us. Depression is a serious problem that affects a person as a whole. Some people may slip into depression with a single incident in life, while others may deal with it more frequently. Sadness, anger, hopelessness, mood swings, anxiety, trouble concentrating, changes in eating habits, change in appearance, being overwhelmed by life, a loss of interest in people and things you once were fond of, and even thoughts of suicide can all be linked to depression. Depression is a serious matter that should be recognized and handled quickly.

Can Depression Be Treated?

The treatment for depression can include one or several treatments to overcome it. Antidepressant medications, along with psychotherapy, are used to help with depression when prescribed by a doctor or physician. Psychotherapy is a form of therapy that focuses on an individuals' views about themselves and the world around them. It involves detecting any difficulties in life they have encountered and showing the patients ways to help them avoid them. Though medication and psychotherapy can help in the treatment of depression, is it enough to get rid of it for good?

There is a choice to go with prescribed medications from a physician, which can cost a lot of money for temporary relief and not a permanent cure. The medications also come with side effects, and there is a possibility that you will become addicted to the medications or drugs prescribed to you. Dependence on medication is another problem other than the depression that can develop. The person dealing with depression may start to depend on the medication much. Then, the medication is no longer a drug for a cure, but it rather becomes a poison to the body. So medication is not really the answer to depression.

Attending sessions in psychotherapy can be a good outlet for people dealing with depression, as it's always good to talk someone, especially a trained therapist about your depression. But is talking to psychotherapist going to cure your depression permanently or is it just a temporary relief? The psychotherapist has to end the session at some point, as each session has a starting and ending time. Though it may seem like your depression is compressed, eventually, the condition will return, and the psychotherapist cannot be by your side for every bout of your depression. It would be wrong to say that medication and psychotherapy is not helpful when it comes to depression, but both remedies should not be depended on entirely. Doping yourself up with drugs and putting all your hope in another human being, who has their own problems in life as well, is not an option for a permanent cure.

The Cure for Depression

For every problem we come across in life, there is always an answer to solve it. For every disease, there is a cure, including depression. All diseases are brought upon ourselves by us. Yes, we can blame Adam and Eve for eating from the tree of good and evil, bringing sin and diseases to a perfect world, but we might have made the decision also if we were in their shoes. The reason why I say so is because humanity is committing and indulging in sin today. Present-day medications for depression has come to be equated to God itself today, as people entirely rely on doctors and pharmaceutical corporations to heal them. As soon as we catch the flu or so, we run to the nearest drug store for Nyquil or some other medicine. If all diseases and conditions, such as depression, are caused by our disobedience, then why did Christ conquer sin at the cross on Calvary? Let's take a look at Isaiah 53:5.

"But he was pierced for our rebellion, crushed for our sins. He was beaten so we could be whole. He was whipped so we could be healed." (Isa 53:5)

This verse assured us physical and mental healing long before Jesus Christ died for our sins and sickness. Jesus Christ is the best doctor, best-prescribed medication, and best therapist and that too one the world cannot offer. He is not temporary, but permanent. He was the same yesterday, is today, and will be forever. (Heb 13:8). The Holy Bible has many instances of Christ healing people and performing miracles, such as healing a blind man and a leper, casting demons out of people, and even raised Lazarus from the dead. So, do you think it is impossible for Christ to heal your depression? Jesus Christ is the cure for depression and any sickness in the world.

Prayer

Dear heavenly Father, I know depression is an awful illness that can keep me locked inside the prison of my mind. I know depression can harm me mentally, psychologically, and emotionally. How grateful I am that you sent Your Son Jesus Christ to conquer all sins and diseases. When depression comes my way Lord, remind me to open my Holy Bible and direct me to the scriptures that will encourage and motivate me. Lord, I ask that You be with me and others to bring us peace and be with us so we will not fall into depression. Help us to think nothing but about the blessings You have given us instead of our mistakes and problems. Your love is everlasting and how thankful and glad I am for your mercy. Thank You, Lord, for everything you have done for me. I give praise, glory, and honor. In Jesus' name, I pray. Amen.

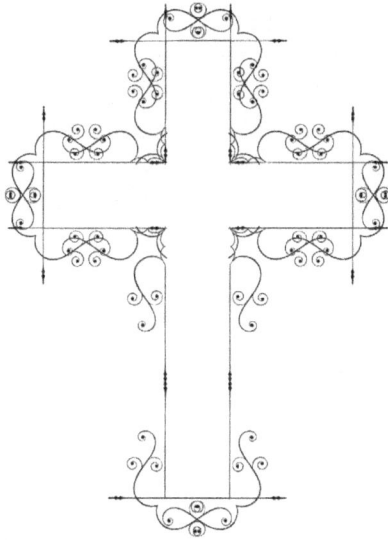

CHAPTER 6: DRUGS & ALCOHOL RUIN LIVES

"Speed Kills, Slow Down and live."

—Anton C. Sears

"Come on, have a drink, Anton; it's not going to hurt," said my big cousin Donte on New Year's Eve, 2002. I was 18 years old at the time. I have never had any alcohol before—no liquor, wine, or beer. Going into a New Year, my family always had fun and drank at family gatherings, and it was like a ritual. Finally, after refusing Donte many times, I accepted his offer, and he handed me a glass of Bacardi Limon. The lemon flavor made it a lot easier to drink, as I almost choked on my first sip. As the taste of Bacardi Limon became tolerable, sips became gulps, and it left me passed out on the floor for hours that night. The next day, I was the joke of the family. I was told about all the funny and weird things I did the night before, and I couldn't remember any of it. If I couldn't remember any of what I did, it meant that I was so out of control the night before. I wondered if it wasn't me controlling my actions the night before, then what was in control of my mind and body? But, the pounding headache that came with the hangover reminded me that a fun night of drinking comes along with it. With the memory loss and the hangover and the terrible taste of the liquor, you would have thought I would never touch alcohol again. Only if you knew that it was only my coming out party. As alcohol began to be a part of my life, marijuana also came into the picture. However, I soon realized it was not my thing. Smoking marijuana, cigarettes, or anything else of the sort affected my stamina, and I loved to play sports.

Why Do People Drink
Going back to when I started drinking at the age of 18, I realize myself along with the other teenagers today share similar reasons on why we began to start drinking and why it continued as we got older.

Being under the age of 21, drinking seemed so cool. It brought a feeling of being grown up, even though I surely didn't look very grown up at the time. I enjoyed drinking, but I cannot not factor in the role peer pressure had in getting me started. My curiosity and desire to know how it felt to drink and be drunk led to me begin experimenting with alcohol.

Boredom was another reason, as I became idle my mind began to wonder. Boredom can lead to all kinds of trouble. An idle mind can be an open playing field for the Devil's temptations, as the mind is not at work and occupied. It gives Satan an opportunity to manipulate the idle mind as boredom takes it course.

Self-Medication was yet another reason. When I felt low and was dealing with emotional and stress problems, I resorted to alcohol for comfort. It led me to rely on alcohol as a medication to temporarily ease the pain and escape the problems I was dealing with. I thought it was what I needed day in and day out. It became so bad that it seemed like I couldn't function without it. I just followed my parents' behavior—not that they abused alcohol, they just liked to have fun. As I grew up seeing it, I followed suit. As my parents were regular drinkers, I also had easy access to their stash.

My ignorance also contributed to me starting to drink. When I started drinking, I was a teenager, and I experimented and felt obligated to do so. The act of experimenting is not innocent or harmless. As I saw my friends and family drinking, it felt like I was going to miss out on all the fun if I didn't drink. I drank to have fun, and getting drunk with my friends was fun. It was so much fun that it became a weekend ritual. The wild behavior, slurred words, and the goofiness were all very enjoyable and created great memories. It is all fun until someone is seriously injured or in court about to get sentenced to jail or pronounced dead due to the recklessness brought about by drinking. I had become addicted to alcohol. I never thought I would get addicted when I started drinking. But it happened when alcohol become a part of my lifestyle. Being addicted to alcohol can take a toll on your body. For instance, it increases the rate of ageing; imagine being 21 and looking like a 40-year old. Alcohol weakens your immune system, leaving your body prone to diseases. Addiction to alcohol can also affect the heart adversely, causing problems such as strokes and high blood pressure. Alcohol can also affect the way the brain works, as it affects the brain communication pathway.

Drunkenness is a sin (Eph 5:18). The Holy Bible doesn't tell you not to drink, but it warns you about the dangers of its abuse. Some might take the instance of Christ's first miracle of turning water into wine in John, Chapter 2, and say that Jesus drank wine and promoted drunkenness. There is no proof that Christ drank wine at the Jewish wedding where he performed the miracle. It would contradict his character as Christ was thought to be throughout the New Testament. Moreover, Christ thought that drunkards would not inherit the kingdom of God (Gal 5:21).

"Wine produces mockers; alcohol leads to brawls. Those lead astray by drink cannot be wise." (Prov 20:1)

The Harm in Using Drugs
If alcohol isn't doing enough damage to people and ruining their lives, drugs pick up the slack as both alcohol and drugs are partners in crime. Illegal drugs include cocaine, speed, marijuana (marijuana can be helpful to patients with medical conditions, but it is still illegal in some states), heroin, ecstasy, Meth, shrooms, acid, to name a few. Another drug to be aware of in the world is the date rape drug. The date rape drug is around the size of an aspirin. It is primarily used for sexual assault, as it can be easily put into someone's beverage, causing the victim to have temporary memory loss. The Holy Bible doesn't

address any form of rules related to drug use. However, just because the Holy Bible doesn't prohibit the use of illegal drugs, is it all right to use them?

Let's take a look at Romans 13:1-2.

"Everyone must submit to governing authorities. For all authority comes from God, and those in positions of authority have been placed there by God. So anyone who rebels against authority is rebelling against what God has instituted, and they will be punished."

God calls all humanity to respect authority to enable good living standards in the society. If rules are broken, such as that on the use of illegal substances (drugs), it can lead to serving jail time; moreover, you're harming yourself in the process. Just like alcohol, drugs put the whole body at risk. Drugs affect your moods, judgement, decision-making and learning abilities and can cause memory loss. Drugs cause sickness, depression, hallucinations, and kidney and liver problems. Different drugs have different effects on the body. Drugs that are consumed through smoking can lead to heart problems and lung and mouth cancers. Drugs such as cocaine, meth, and others that use a needle for injection is an easy way to catch HIV/AIDS. Overall, drugs kill people; so, why take them?

Being a correctional officer, I have witnessed young adults coming to jail addicted to drugs and have heard the news of their deaths from an overdose weeks after being released from jail. Drugs can destroy your health, not just physically but mentally and emotionally too.

Respect Your Body

Now that we know that alcohol and drugs can harm our bodies and kill us, is it a smart choice to give ourselves to them? Many teenagers believe that they have the freedom to do as they please because technically it is their bodies often hiding their bad habits from their parents. However, many think so unknowingly become enslaved to their own desires and habits.

The apostle Paul states, in 1 Corinthians 6:20, that we must honor God with our bodies. God created each and every one of us; I don't think God wants us to poison our body, corrupting his intelligent design. Remember, he handcrafted you. Let me put it like this—if you stayed in an apartment or building owned by someone else, you would try the best not to violate the rules of the building. Violating the rules or laws of anything owned by someone comes with consequences. As God is our creator, our bodies belong to him, and we must not violate the standards of living He has set for us. Our relationship with God was already once violated.

God brought us back with the high price of sacrificing His Son Jesus Christ for our sins and the acts of Satan. Don't give yourself into your sinful desires; when temptation strikes, pick up your bible and read or seek godly counsel. We are all imperfect human beings who will and are going to make mistakes in life. Let's just make sure we learn from them before the mistakes cause be our downfall. Trust me, if you submit yourself to God, Satan will flee (Jam 4:7).

Drugs and alcohol have been killing teenagers and young adults for years, and now the situation is getting worse more than ever. Don't allow yourself to be a victim; respect your body. Know that God loves you, and, most of all, honor your body before God.

Prayer

Dear heavenly Father, thank You for all that You have done and provided for me while on earth. Father, the world You have created, and the people in it have fallen victim to alcohol and drugs. I pray that all teenagers and young adults do not get swayed to use alcohol or drugs, and they are delivered from the oppression of man (drug dealers and alcoholics). Father, when sickness comes, remind me to depend on Your healing power and not any medication that could lead me to addiction. For the rest of the time that You allow me to walk this earth Lord, may I respect and honor my body that You created for your glorification. Father, I love You and thank You for everything You have done for me. I give You praise, glory, and honor. In Jesus' mighty name, I pray. Amen.

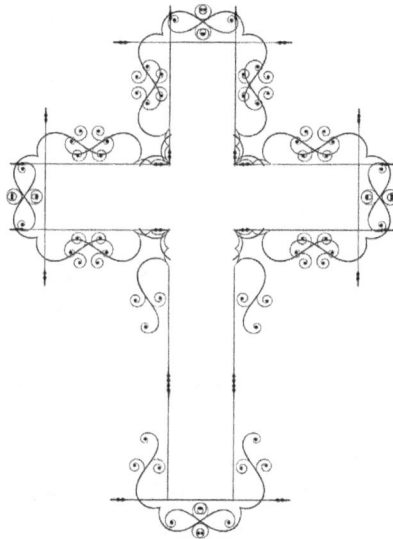

CHAPTER 7: HATRED, RACISM & VIOLENCE

If God loves everyone and is omnipresent (present in all places), omniscient (all-knowing), and omnipotent (all-powerful), then why does He allow hatred, racism, and violence continue to ruin the world? The truth is that God is aware of the hatred, racism, and violence in the world, and He is going to do something about it (2 Pet 3:12-13). The world is broken, and humanity is trying to fix it on its own not knowing that the humanity is broken within themselves and that two negatives don't make a positive. God created this world perfectly without hatred, racism, or violence in it. God gave his creation free will to choose. However, the freedom to choose brought pain and suffering into the world.

The world we live in is no longer the world God created perfectly. It is Satan who is the God of this world now (2 Cor 4:4). Nonetheless, God is superior to Satan.

Satan was God's highest-ranking angel once and one of God most beautiful creations. Satan was not pleased with his position, so he desired to be God and not a servant of God and to take over as the ruler of the universe. God then cast Satan down from heaven due to his pride (Isa14:12-15). Days, months, or maybe years later, Satan tempted Adam and Eve to eat from the tree of knowledge, corrupting God's perfect world, resulting in what I like to call the fall of humanity. All the evil in the world that manifests as hatred, racism, and violence throughout the world comes from the mastermind of Satan. He does not make us perform the actions but is able to influence and infatuate our minds, using humanity for his dirty work to ruin the lives of others and everything God says is good. When evil happens, we tend to blame God for it instead of blaming the Satan for his influences that lead to our wrongdoings. Satan's greatest trick is to convince to humanity that he does not exist.

Racism Divides God's People

One thing I hate besides Satan is racism—seeing God's creation abuse, fight, and kill each other because of skin color. Racism is prejudice and discrimination directed against someone of a different people group based on the belief that one's own group is more superior than the other. The color of our skin doesn't make us better than another person. God created people of all color equal, and none is above the other.

In my life, I have stereotyped people of different color, and it's wrong because I didn't even know them. While some of the stereotyping could have been true, it still doesn't give me an excuse to alienate people who are of a different skin color than me. Stereotyping is a huge problem all around the world, as people judge others by their appearance. I love the simple fact that God doesn't judge us by appearance but by our hearts (1 Sam 16:7). Appearance does not override the character of a person. If the people in the society were to judge others by their heart and not their appearance, the society would get along much better.

We have all had bad encounters in life related to racial bias irrespective of whether you were labeled a name based on your color, fought over an event in the world that you had nothing to do with, or defended yourself for being outside of your neighborhood. Racism is a serious worldwide issue and causes panic throughout the world. Racism causes hate crimes such as racial harassment and murder. The hate people have for each other is destroying the world, and with all the hate and violence going on, Satan is sitting back and applauding the acts of his puppets as they continue to do his dirty work on earth.

Separation From the Body of Christ

Months after I gave my life to Christ, I joined The House of Elohim In Jesus Christ, my first home church. It was located in a place that used to be a shopping mall. There were around fifteen to twenty other churches in the compound. The members of my church were primarily African Americans. It wasn't the church policy for only African Americans to join the church, but they chose to join the church mostly at the time. The other churches primarily had an all-white population, and some others had mixed groups. I never understood why we were separated from each other and not unified if we were all followers of Christ and members in the body of Christ (1 Cor 12:27). It seemed like all the churches were competing against each other. I just couldn't imagine the impact that could be made in the community or the world if all churches came together. The current home church that my family and I attend has members from diverse backgrounds, and I love it for that simple fact. It has around 150 to 200 people attending church service each Sunday. Now with so many professing Christians in the building, the love of Christ should be flowing. At times it can be awkward when you walk up and speak to the people in the church, and, in return, you get a silent treatment or notice the same person each Sunday and seem like total strangers to each other.

The point I'm trying to make here is that only the love of God can conquer the evil and wrath of racism in the world. If Christians can't show fellow brothers and sisters in Christ the love of God, how can we ever try to make a difference in the world that doesn't know Jesus Christ? Therefore, though there are many who don't believe in Christ, we have to live through Christ in order to make a difference so that they see his love through us.

A professing Christian should not be afraid to look and examine their own hearts to see their views of other people both directly or indirectly to develop relationships with people of different color. This world that is racially divided will never be a world that God is pleased with. God's love for people of all color is evident in the Holy Bible.

Let's take a look at Revelation 7:9-10.

"After this I saw a vast crowd, too great to count, from every nation and tribe and people and language, standing in front of the throne and before the Lamb. They were clothed in white robes and held palm branches in their hands. And they were shouting with a great roar, Salvation comes from our God who sits on the throne and from the Lamb!"

In the above verses, Christ doesn't specifically say Whites, Blacks, or Hispanics group; instead he includes every nation, tribe, people, and language. How beautiful would it be to see the world coming together—united and one. A world where diverse people of all color stand side by side without any hatred, violence, or racism, but the way God had intended them to be—in love. No one is born filled with hatred, violence, and racism; instead, the differentiation based on color is taught to them. In the Holy Bible, there are no categories of Black or White churches, as Christ didn't come to save your skin color but to save souls.

"For the Son of man is come to save that which was lost." (Matt 18:11)

If our mindsets are outdated, there is no way WE, as God's people and nation, come together and move forward to the future. 2000 years ago, Christ ended the question regarding which lives are the most superior in the world. He died for people of all color. ALL LIVES MATTER TO GOD.

Prayer

Dear heavenly Father, thank You for all that You have provided me. I come to You Father, sad and deeply hurt by the hatred and violence caused by racism. I understand that we struggle not just against flesh and blood but against powers and principalities too. Father, racism is being kept alive by continuing the lie that certain creations of Yours are more superior than the others based on skin color. Please give us the strength and grace to free ourselves of racial stereotypes, which abuse some of us while giving entitlements to others. Father, help us create a nation that embraces the hopes and fears of the abused people of color in our society and all around the world. Father, I thank You and love You for being God, the creator of my universe. I give You all praise, glory, and honor. Amen.

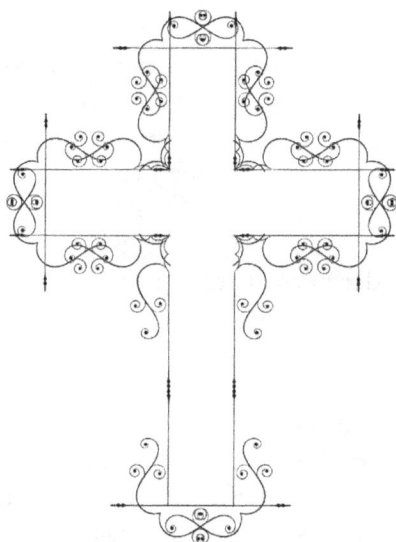

CHAPTER 8: PRESSURE BURSTS PIPES

"Don't copy the behavior and customs of this world, but let God transform you into a new person by changing the way you think. Then you will learn to know God`s will for you, which is good and pleasing and perfect."

—Romans 12:2

The teenage years of our lives are when we start to present ourselves to the world. Teenage years are the beginning years of one becoming independent. At the age of 14, I started to work at McDonald's. I caught the bus to and from destinations on my own. I kept myself groomed, as it was now my responsibility to get my own haircuts. The things my Mom and Dad used to do for me became my responsibility, as I learned to take care of myself. During your teenage years, as you get the freedom to explore and begin to see new things in life, you tend to develop your own ideas and principles that shape your personality into the person you want to be. You also tend to be influenced by those you spend time with the most.

In my teenage years, spending all summer with my friends and others, I started to imitate my friends, and later on, I started to

ANTON C. SEARS

influenced by them. I didn't want to be the corny, nerdy, lame guy, as I was often called. I wanted my friends and others to see me to be cool, and I just wanted to fit in. The more and more I crumbled under the peer pressure to be cool, the more I drifted away from the person I used to be. I turned into a jock puppet who could be controlled by the strings held by my peers. As time passed, I slowly began started piecing myself together again and redefining a new me, shedding older personalities, not pleasing my peers anymore. Instead, I allowed God to do a makeover on me to please him and become the person He designed me to be.

Peer pressure can bring the best or the worst out of us. Peer pressure is the pressure from peers to act in a certain way and follow their values to be accepted by them, and it is something we all have experienced in our lives. Peer pressure makes you follow in the same direction as others, and it's easy to follow the bad habits of others, picking up their habits such as smoking, drinking, gambling, and stealing, as the world has turned away from God's morals and values. Most of us do not like to be disliked or rejected by our peers, so we support undesirable causes so that we can fit in with the crowd. Peer pressure leads you away from the person that you really are and can leave scars for the rest of your life. Therefore, the negative side of peer pressure is that it allows others to dictate the person they want you to be, leading you to make wrong choices in life.

Pontius Pilate is a great example of someone who succumbed to peer pressure in the Holy Bible. Let's take a look at Matthew 27:11-26.

"Now Jesus was standing before Pilate, the Roman governor. 'Are you the king of the Jews?' the governor asked him."

Jesus replied, 'You have said it.'

But when the leading priests and the elders made their accusations against him, Jesus remained silent. 'Don't you hear all these charges they are bringing against you?' Pilate demanded. But Jesus made no response to any of the charges, much to the governor's surprise. Now it was the governor's custom each year during the Passover celebration to release one prisoner to the crowd-anyone they wanted. This year there was a notorious prisoner, a man named Barabbas. * As the crowds gathered before Pilate's house that morning, he asked them, 'Which one do you want me to release to you-Barabbas, or Jesus who is called the Messiah?' (He knew very well that the religious leader had arrested Jesus out of envy.) Just then, as Pilate was sitting on the judgment seat, his wife sent him this message: 'Leave that innocent man alone. I suffered through a terrible nightmare about him last night.' Meanwhile, the leading priests and the elders persuaded the crowd to ask for Barabbas to be released and for Jesus to be put to death. So the governor asked again, 'Which of these two do you want me to release to you?'

The crowd shouted back, 'Barabbas!'

Pilate responded, 'Then what should I do with Jesus who is called the Messiah?'

They shouted back, 'Crucify him!'

'Why?' Pilate demanded. 'What crime has he committed?'

But the mob roared even louder, 'Crucify him!'

Pilate saw that he wasn't getting anywhere and that a riot was developing. So, he sent for a bowl of water and washed his hands before the crowd, saying, 'I am innocent of this man's blood. The responsibility is yours!'

And all the people yelled back, 'We will take responsibility for his death-we and our children!'*

So, Pilate released Barabbas to them. He ordered Jesus flogged with a lead-tipped whip, then turned him over to the Roman soldiers to be crucified."

Pontius Pilate knew that Jesus Christ was innocent and that he had committed no crime, as he was blasphemously and falsely accused. Pontius Pilate still decided to let Barabbas, a murderer, go free with no strings attached. Pontius Pilate was stuck between a rock and a hard place. He did not follow his true inclination and judgement to free Jesus Christ and made a safe decision that pleased the people to keep himself in the right terms with them. The situation and response of Pontius Pilate in the above verses demonstrate how we respond under the pressure of our peers. When making decisions based on the desires of our peers, we compromise our better judgement thinking that it's a win-win situation for us, but it's not.

Peer Pressure Can Also Be a Positive

Not all peer pressure is negative. Peer pressure can also help reexamine yourself, your views, and your ways of living. Remember, you are in control to decide whether the outcome of the pressure from your peers is going to be positive or negative. Just like you can please others by saying "Yes," you can please yourself by saying "No" to others. It can be very hard to say "No" to someone we really enjoy being around or look up to. But the decision to follow and please them doesn't improve you. In life, you should make changes to better yourself; if you feel you don't know how to make those necessary changes to improve yourself, then you can start by seeing how other people portray themselves and take inspiration from positive influences. A positive role model can play a vital role in reinventing your personality. If you are blessed to come across a good group of peers, it can be very helpful also. Just like peers can negatively influence you, they can also positively influence you to adopt good habits, such as respecting others, avoiding alcohol and drugs, trying out for a sport you have wanted to play, improving your self-confidence. Overall, positive influence basically encourages you to undertake something that's in your best interests.

After I finished high school, I had made the decision to not undertake higher education. I hated school and had no desire to further my education by going to college. My wife, family, and friends continued to pressure me to continue my education. I felt that I was too old to go back to school and that I would give it up because it would be too hard for me. Their peer pressure helped me find the courage to go back to school. In October 2015, I enrolled in the Liberty University Online for an undergraduate program to obtain my Christian Ministry Certificate. And who would've known that I would go on to finish all the six courses with five As and one B. I received my Christian Ministry Certificate in August 2016. Receiving the certificate was one of the most memorable moments in my life. I thought I'd be a failure if I went back to school, but the pressure from my peers pushed me to not only go back to school but also succeed with flying colors. I am so glad that God influenced them to pressure me to do something I never thought would be possible. Positive peer pressure played a major role in my life when my family and friends looked out for what they thought was best for me and that overshadowed my negative thoughts about going back to school. In this world, if you don't control your own mind, someone else will. You should not be afraid of losing people who do not have your best interests in mind but be afraid of losing yourself trying to please others.

Prayer

Dear heavenly Father, I come to You enduring much pressure from others about how I should act, look, or be. I know You created me like no other in this world, but I have followed and listened to others and allowed them to dictate how I should be, falling into the trap of negatives influences. You didn't create me to follow others; You created me only to follow You. Lord, help me to be the person You created me to be so that when others pressure or judge me, I shall not be affected. I want to break the cycle of falling into peer pressure. Lord, command me to stop being a victim of it now that I have come to see the best in me and can do all things through Your Son Jesus Christ who strengthens me (Phil 4:13). Lord, thank You for helping me accept myself just the way I am. I'm grateful for all the qualities and appearances You given me that make me who I am. I pray for positive peer pressure from others for encouragement, and in return, I am of help to them as well. Lord with Your power and strength, I will stop giving into things people say and do what is not in my best interest. In Jesus' precious name, I pray. Amen.

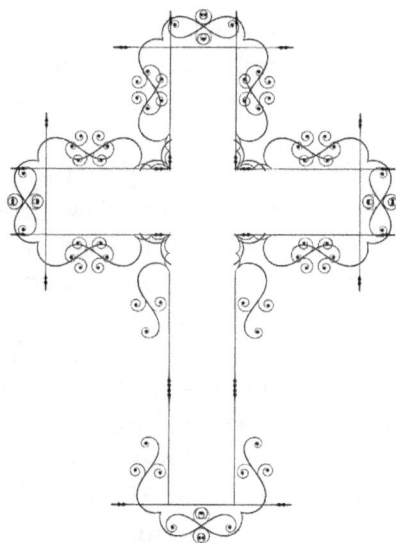

CHAPTER 9: LAZINESS IS A DISEASE

"No Good Things in Life Comes To Those Who Sit and Wait For Them To Happen."

—Anton C. Sears

Laziness can keep one from reaching their purpose in God and missing out on the opportunities in life.

"I'm too lazy to find a job."
"I'm just waiting for someone to motivate me."
"I'm no good at this; I'll try some other time."
"I don't have the inspiration like everyone else does."
"I'm content the way I am."

Laziness is a mood that puts an end to any progress or opportunity that presents itself to us. Laziness can be defined as a failure to do what you are supposed to do, although you have the ability to do so. It doesn't come from something internal that can control us; it's not some kind of gene passed down through our family bloodline, and it's not found in the food and beverages that we consume on a daily basis. Laziness is a lifestyle chosen by some of us, but it is a temptation for all of us. Therefore, laziness is a sin, as God has ordained all of the humanity to work and not to be idle and inactive in life (Gen 2:15).

We are told that working hard pays off at the end, and it is true. But to the lazy person, laziness pays off now. While the person may feel they deserve the desired rest, they slowly start to indulge in it, and finally, laziness begins to become a part of who they are. Honestly, who likes to be around someone lazy? Their laziness can rub off on you, and you will become lazy also. A lazy person wants to reap all the benefits and potential rewards in life but doesn't want to put in the efforts to get them. It's painful for a hard worker to see a person with such an attitude get ahead in life, gaining new jobs or promotions, while you sit and wait for your big break to come. Perhaps you might be dealing with this sort of situation, and you might think your hard work is going unnoticed. Remember, it's not, as God sees everything.

Don't become a Sluggard
A sluggard can be defined as a lazy person, who does not take responsibility for their own life. Now a sluggard and a slug both share something in common. They are both slow moving, and it takes them forever to get somewhere in life. God made slugs to be slow in life, but he did not make people act like slugs. In various scriptures in the book of Proverbs, God has plenty to say about being lazy.

Proverbs 6:9: *"But you, lazybones, how long will you sleep? When will you wake up?"*

Proverbs 10:26: *"Lazy people irritate their employers, like vinegar to the teeth or smoke in the eyes."*

Proverbs 13:4: *"Lazy people want much but get little, but those who work hard will prosper."*

Proverbs 19:24: *"Lazy people take food in their hand but don't even lift it to their mouth."*

Proverbs 20:4: *"Those too lazy to plow in the right season will have no food at the harvest"*

Proverbs 21:25: *"Despite their desires, the lazy will come to ruin, for their hands refuse to work."*

Proverbs 22:13: *"The lazy person claims, "There's a lion out there! If I go outside, I might be killed!"*

Proverbs 26:14 *"As a door swings back and forth on its hinges, so the lazy person turns over in bed."*

God, through the above verses, makes it crystal clear that he is not too fond of a lazy person.

Sluggards miss out on the things God has planned for them in life. God cannot use a lazy person who doesn't want to look out for themselves. They have the ability to work, but they refuse to use it. Instead, they are just happy and do not acknowledge that God has blessed them with a fully functioning body that enables them to work, which not everyone is blessed with. Don't be the one who lacks personal responsibility, drive, and good judgement to provide for your needs. When I was a teenager, my parents always gave me chores around the house such as cleaning my room, taking out the trash, cutting the grass, washing the dishes, among others. There were times when I complained and did the job half-heartedly; so, I received little or no money based on my job performance. Little did I know that I wasn't just working for money but also the food that my parents provided me because if you don't work, you don't eat (2 Thess 3:10). The electricity that I used in the house to play my video games cost money as well. At times, I believed my parents were punishing me with chores, but they were just preparing me to be an adult and work a job that provided for me so that I could be productive in life and not be a sluggard.

Overcoming Laziness

To overcome laziness, the enemy of productivity, you must first find out what's causing you to be lazy. The following are some causes why you may be experiencing laziness:

Procrastination: It is the avoiding of something that must be accomplished. Laziness generally is born when we continue to postpone our tasks in life, thinking we have all the time in the world to get it done. But in all rationality, we come up with the excuse that you can do it later. Why postpone what needs to be done, when you can do it now?

Irresponsibility: It is a state of a person lacking a sense of responsibility. Running away from your responsibilities will make you lazy in your life. Some teenagers and young adults may have the luxury of having parents and guardians who do everything for them, and in the end, they will live irresponsibly when they grow older.

Lack of motivation: Motivation is the desire to find a reason to do something in your life. Motivation is the drive that will lead you to accomplish things in life. If you like school or your job, you will be motivated to do things correctly and keep up a good performance. And if you lack motivation, you will find a million reasons why you can't accomplish things, which can make you lazy.

Lack of Self Worth: Self-worth is thevalue that you give yourself and involves believing in yourself. If you believe in yourself, you will hold yourself to high standards, and that will allow you to get things done in life whether you're at home, work, or school. If you don't value yourself, you will live a lazy life because you don't believe you can do any better.

Distractions: A distraction is something that prevents you from giving your full attention to a task you have undertaken. There are plenty of distractions in the world to keep your mind wandering off the task at hand. In order to not be lazy and get distracted, eliminate what causes you to be distracted when you're performing the task at hand irrespective of whether it's Facebook, Instagram, video games, friends, or upcoming events. Remember, there will always be time for such things, but one shouldn't put them above matters that are more important.

Indecisiveness: Indecisiveness is the characteristic of not being able to make decisions for yourself. When God allows you to wake up in the morning, you have a day full of decisions to make, such as "What should I wear today;" "What should I eat for breakfast;" "Should I try out for the basketball team at school?" Some people cannot make up their minds and decide for themselves, which leaves them confused going back and forth on what they should do leaving them idle. Such situations can foster laziness because they're stuck between a rock and a hard place. Having not made a decision, you have now wasted half or most of your day, and by the time you came up with a decision, it isn't enough time to follow through with the decision you made.

Lack of Sleep: Not getting proper rest can also make you feel lethargic and lazy. How can you be productive with no sleep? Good rest is very important.

Poor Nutrition: The food that you eat plays a big part in your body's energy level. If you do not eat well, your body will lack the energy required for the body to perform well. I know many of us love fast food, but let's be honest, it is not healthy at all. A lot of junk food in your body will leave you feeling weak and rundown. Remember your body is just like a car; if you put a lot of cheap junk into your car, it's bound to break down. So, don't continue to feed your body junk food; give it the nutrition it needs to keep up a high performance.

Benefits: Benefits are the advantages and profits gained in life. One reason you may become lazy in completing the tasks in your life is when you think of how hard it is to complete it instead of looking at the benefits of completing it. Be sure to focus on the benefits of completing a task instead or how difficult the task is.

Regardless of how long you been lazy, laziness can be eliminated from your life. Once you understand what is causing you be a certain way, the easier it is for you to identify what's been holding you back from being productive in life. God wants to be useful you in life; He wants to see His wonderful creation flourish in life because He didn't create you to be useless.

Jesus Christ did not possess any characteristics of laziness. Before his crucifixion, he knew what was in store for him in order to redeem humanity back to its rightful owner (God). Knowing that he would get beaten by men, spit on, whipped with a cat-o-nine, crowned thorns, and most of all, nailed to a cross, Christ could have refused the will his Father in heaven had for him. He could have chosen to not carry out my assignment in life because his Father's creation will continue to be sinful and be disobedient. But Christ was obedient to the will of God, and he accepted it saying, "I want your will to be done, not mine" (Luke 22:42).

Prayer

Dear heavenly Father, thank You for the many blessings You have given me from day to day. You're so loving and understanding; even when am wrong in Your eyes, You still show love towards me. Father, I am sorry that at times I can be lazy. I procrastinate the things in life that need to be done. I have been distracted in life, and that's keeping me off track and from being invaluable to You and myself. Please help me resist my tendency to be lazy so that I can be productive and accomplish all that You created me to. I also pray for others dealing with laziness as well. Laziness doesn't honor or glorify You, Father. I thank You and love You for all that You have done for me. I give You all praise, glory, and honor. In Jesus' mighty name, I pray. Amen

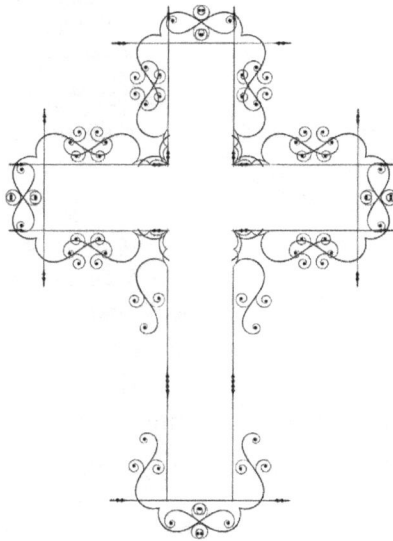

RESISTING SATAN

"So humble yourselves before God. Resist the devil, and he will flee from you."
—James 4:7

Nothing is more satisfying than being able to resist someone, something, or any addictions that harm you and does not add value to your life—someone like Satan who is not some fiery red person with a pitchfork. He comes disguised as everything you have ever fantasized about in life. Satan is like a bad partner you have been dating. You know, the one so popular among all your friends like him, but your parents don't care for. When you spend time with him, he promises you fun and excitement in life (sin). He doesn't value your life, loves you, or promise you a bright future. However, despite his flaws of not caring for you, it's just so hard to resist him because the sins he influences you to do is so enticing that when temptation comes your way you succumb. The Devil uses you in the relationship to fulfil his evil desires and to attract others to him. While dealing with Satan, there's another person in your life who is not so popular with everyone in the world. This person values you, loves you for who you are and has a bright future for you, and his name is Jesus Christ. Some people fail to realize that in the life they are leading, they're either serving Satan or God in all that they do. Many may disagree with this statement depending on their views in life. The choices and actions in your life are either righteous or unrighteous and influenced by Satan or God. So, is Satan really a friend or enemy?

The Devil's Schemes

Once you move away from Satan on to bigger and better things and a better relationship with God, he becomes your enemy, as he is the enemy of God who wants you back just like a jealous partner you broke up within a previous relationship. He will do any and everything to get you back and try to destroy you. As you and the Devil are now ex-partners and enemies now, it's important that you learn all his schemes so that you will not fall for him again.

Remember, Satan lies and is the father of all lies.

"For you are the children of your father the devil, and you love to do the evil things he does. He was a murderer from the beginning. He has always hated the truth because there is no truth in him. When he lies, it is consistent with his character; for he is a liar and the father of lies." (John 8:44)

The Devil also known as Satan made his first appearance in Genesis, Chapter 3. He had a conversation with Eve about the fruits of the tree of good and evil and led Eve to disobey God, bringing sin into the world; it all started with the lies of the Devil.

Satan blinds the minds of those who don't believe in God.

"Satan, who is the god of this world, has blinded the minds of those who don't believe in him. They are unable to see the glorious light of the Good News. They don't understand this message about the glory of Christ, who is the exact likeness of God." (2 Cor 4:4)

If you do not recognize that there is an all-powerful God who created the world and everything in it, it's easy for Satan to blind people. Because if they don't believe in God, they don't believe in Satan as well. Satan's greatest trick is to convince humanity that he doesn't exist.

Satan uses other people as devices to deceive others by appearing to be attractive and good. The Devil also has servants just like God does. They profess lies that come off as the truth of God to lead others astray away from God so that you wouldn't know the truth and teach others the same. Jesus says "Beware of false prophets who come disguised as harmless sheep but are really vicious wolves." (Matt 7:15)

You can spot these false prophets by their teachings, as they are motivated by power, popularity, or money. Moreover, they tend to glorify themselves over Christ.

Satan tempts you to sin.

Satan sets the stage but doesn't make you do anything. If we sin, we do it because we have chosen do so. In the garden of Eden, he enticed Eve by influencing her thoughts. He is very devious and has caused all of us to sin. However, there is one person—Jesus Christ—who protects your thoughts (Matt 4:1-11). The Devil only gives you the invitation to sin; you don't have to accept it.

Satan tries to take away the word of God so that you denounce your faith in Christ.

Before Satan tempted Eve in the garden of Eden, he first challenged the word of God (Gen 3:1-6). If you're not one hundred percent sure that the Holy Bible is true, it gives him the chance to make you doubt your beliefs about God.

Satan causes sickness and diseases in the world.

On the sixth day of creation, "God looked over all he had made, and he saw that it was very good" (Gen 1:31). So, the world was perfect until sin came in the world. And with sin came all types of sickness and diseases people have today. So, the Devil is to be blamed even for all the natural disasters that happen around the world.

Satan is a murderer.

Satan is evil. He is out for blood. Christ came into the world so that we can have a life. On the contrary, Satan's purpose is to make life a living hell and destroy all that he can.

Satan is very smart and clever, and he is humanity's greatest enemy. Peter states that "Stay alert! Watch out for your great enemy, the devil. He prowls around like a roaring lion, looking for someone to devour" (1 Pet 5:8). The best way to attack somebody is when they are alone, as that's when they are the most vulnerable. This is the same method that the Devil uses. The best way to fight Satan is with the word of God (Holy Bible) just as Christ did in Matthew 4:11. Satan is smart, but he is no match for the power of God, and God's word has power.

"For the word of God is alive and powerful. It is sharper than the sharpest two-edged sword, cutting between soul and spirit, between joint and marrow. It exposes our innermost thoughts and desires" (Heb 4:12).

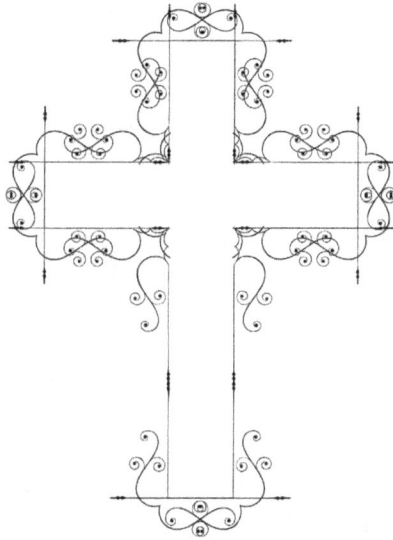

VICTORY IN CHRIST

The more real Satan appears in the world today; the more amazing the victory of Christ comes to those who believe in him. Living in this world and battling Satan is like the unlimited rounds of boxing inside a ring; some rounds will be won, and some rounds will be lost. When defeats happen, understand that it's all right, as no one has a perfect record of against fighting Satan and his demons. The defeats will not have an effect on your outcome in life. It is Christ saying that you cannot defeat this adversary alone, and you need him. Fighting his attacks and achieving temporary victories over him only comes through the faith in Jesus Christ. So like any enemy you have encountered before, it's time to start discovering ways to be victorious over Satan.

1.Understand Your Enemy

There is an old saying "Keep your friends close and your enemies closer," which I believe is true. The Devil wants to destroy you, so it's important that you understand him. You need to know what he's capable of doing and his limitations and weaknesses.

"Put on all of God's armor so that you will be able to stand firm against all

59

strategies of the devil." (Eph 6:11)

2. Know the Devil's Methods
Know how he works and operates; you cannot not be uneducated when it comes to his methods.

"So that Satan will not outsmart us. For we are familiar with his evil schemes." (2 Cor 2:11)

3. Know All Those Among You
The Devil uses other people as his devices to corrupt; so, be mindful of others.

"Dear friends, do not believe everyone who claims to speak by the Spirit. You must test them to see if the spirit they have comes from God. For there are many false prophets in the world." (1 John 4:11)

4. Be Alert!
Satan is very tricky and cunning; he can deceive even the best. You should be on your guard at all times.

"Stay alert! Watch out for your great enemy, the devil. He prowls around like a roaring lion, looking for someone to devour." (1 Pet 5:8)

5. Resist Satan When He Comes Your Way
When Satan tried to tempt Jesus Christ in the desert, Christ fought back with the word of God. Stand your ground rely on God's word and power, and he will flee.

"So humble yourselves before God. Resist the devil, and he will flee from you." (Jam 4:7)

6. Understand Your Weaknesses
Everyone is vulnerable to something. The Devil knows your weaknesses. Not knowing what we shouldn't give him, gives him the chance to exploit them.

"The temptations in your life are no different from what others experience. And God is faithful. He will not allow the temptation to be more than you can

stand. When you are tempted, he will show you a way out so that you can endure." (1 Cor 10:13)

7. Do Not Rely on Your Strength But God's Strength Only
You shouldn't underestimate the power of the Devil. It would be foolish to fight the Devil without relying on God.

"But even Michael, one of the mightiest of the angels, did not dare accuse the devil of blasphemy, but simply said, 'The Lord rebuke you!'" (Jude 9)

8. Run from the Situation
Avoid any situation that tempts you to sin or causes you to sin. Separate yourself away from the causes of sin.

"Stay away from every kind of evil." (1 Thess 5:22)

Satan only has a short time on earth (Rev 12:12), so he is moving fast to destroy who love Christ and deceive others. So, the above steps will help you in fighting Satan. Satan is already defeated from the work Christ did on Calvary. You must live in the victory of Christ, knowing that the Satan is already a defeated foe.

Prayer
Dear heavenly Father, I'm so thankful that the Devil is already defeated. I praise You Father for what Your Son my Lord and Savior Jesus Christ has done in his sinless life, death, and resurrection. Even though the Devil only has a short while on this earth, I rejoice in knowing that I already have the victory over him through Jesus Christ. Father, I also pray in Jesus' name to bind any spirit that is not Yours whether it's anger, wrath, murder, hatred, violence, jealousy, envy, pride, criticism, complaining, or false teaching. Father, I'm looking forward to the day Christ reigns and take over the world. I will pray in the name of the Lord Jesus Christ when the Devil and his demons try to destroy the plans You have for my life. I love You and thank You for all that you have done for me. I give you all praise, glory, and honor. In Jesus' name, I pray. Amen.

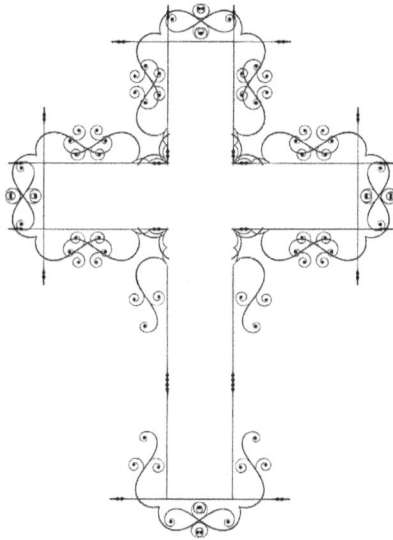

GOD IS LOVE

"But anyone who does not love does not know God, for God is love."

—1 John 4:8

Suppose you grew up in a home where no matter how good you did or performed in life, you were never really sure you were loved by your family. You tried so hard to get the attention of those that you loved, and they never had the time to spend with you because of their busy schedules. As you secured good grades in school and achieved your goals in life, you received the best gifts anybody could ask for. When the times were hard, and you needed someone to talk to, you were given get well soon cards with the writing inside saying "I Love You". And the way they showed love to you never really seemed meaningful to you. So, you always felt heavy in your heart because you were never quite sure if you were loved. Therefore, you always wondered, "Does anyone in the world love me? Why can't no one ever spend time with me? Is love nothing but being showered by a bunch of gifts?"

Growing up not knowing what love is can affect you because you might feel you were never really loved. Sadly, most people in the

63

world don't know what true love is or where it comes from. Humanity defines love by their feelings or emotions, and both can change any moment. The world portrays love as being conditional. Maybe, that's one reason why we see so many divorces these days. They love each other one day, and then they stop loving each other and decide to call it quits.

The Merriam-Webster dictionary defines love as "a feeling of strong or constant affection for a person." "Constant affection" often comes from having a sexual attraction to another person. Attraction to another person is not love; we are just attracted to them primarily because they make us feel good. We live in a world that confuses love for lust.

One morning, I decided to go to the gym to workout. I was at the Fitness 19 gym, and loud music was playing on the radio, which everyone in the whole building could hear. The song being played was Rihanna's "We Found Love". The Chorus to the song went like this, "We found love in a hopeless place". It repeated a number of times until the lyrics of the song started. The beat of the song was very catchy to the point you would tune out the lyrics. So, when I heard the chorus, I automatically thought of the people in the world who doesn't know what true love is and has it all confused. People feel that they have found love when they feel a strong attraction to someone else. This world is filled with pornography, drugs, and alcohol, and people are looking for love in all the wrong places.

True Love Only Found in God
The world has contaminated love by the misconceptions and misunderstandings about it. Love is selflessness and does not look out for only one's interest. In order to understand the true meaning of love, we must find the source of it. If we compare the world's views on love against what the Holy Bible has to say about it, we discover that love is not a feeling, not an emotion, not an attraction, not having sex, not liking someone, but love is a moral character, and it's a choice. The Holy Bible shows that moral character of God through Jesus Christ. Throughout the Holy Bible, God shows that His love based on His character. Let's take at some scripture verses that show God is the basis of love.

"For God loved the world so much that he gave his one and only Son so that everyone who believes in him will not perish but have eternal life." (John 3:16)

"But God showed his great love for us by sending Christ to die for us while we were still sinners."

-Rom 5:8

"So humble yourselves under the mighty power of God, and at the right time he will lift you up in honor. Give all your worries and care to God, for he cares about you."

-1 Pet 5:6-7

True love is unconditional, as it's more concerned with the needs of others than with oneself. You can tell someone that you love them, but your actions should speak the same in the way you act and treat them. A perfect definition of God's love can be found in 1 Corinthians 13:4-7.

"Love is patient and kind. Love is not jealous or boastful or proud. Or rude. It does not demand its own way. It is not irritable, and it keeps no record of being wronged. It does not rejoice about injustice but rejoices whenever the truth wins out. Love never gives up, never loses faith, is always hopeful, and endures through every circumstance."

God is love, and love is not God. Without God, we cannot love at all. Love is the greatest gift God has given humanity, and that gift is Jesus Christ. God doesn't love us because we are lovable but because he first loved us. I repented and accepted Jesus Christ as my Lord and Savior not because of how I felt, or it was the right thing to do. I made the choice, and I finally decided to give up my sinful life so that I can live for Jesus Christ. Love makes you selfless; love will make you sacrificing; love will make you transform the person you use to be. Love is very powerful, as it can break barriers. It will make you love even your enemies, as you have a new outlook on life.

God's love for us is the reason why Christ died on the cross. God's love for those who put their trust in Christ is why he holds them dearly and will never let them go. God's love is the reason why I wrote this book. Listen, God loves you. In life, we often venture out and try new things. So why not try God.

Prayer

Dear heavenly Father, thank You for loving me so much. Even when I violate Your standards of living, You still love me. For the most of my life, I have had the wrong understanding of love and carried it out the wrong way. Father, I am sorry for all those I have hurt and wronged with the excuse of "Love". I understand now that it cannot be earned from the approval of anyone, but it can only be truly obtained from You. Thank You for making me and the fallen world realize the real meaning of what true love is through Your Son Christ Jesus and Your word (The Holy Bible). Father, may I never be drawn to the wrong perception of love but gain understanding and confidence through Your Son Jesus Christ.

I could never give You what You have given the world through Your Son Jesus Christ, but I can honor you with the life I live. Father, I thank You and love You. I give you all praise, glory, and honor. In Jesus' precious name, I pray. Amen.

CONCLUSION

To be led to something greater, we must recognize the danger we're currently in. God wants you to be reunited with to him, but to do so, you must make the decision yourself. We are all tempted by Satan, and we all fail in life—that's just part of life. Your life may not be what you want it to be, but that doesn't give you reason to waste it. God has you here in the world for a reason. You may not know it now, but trust me—bind in him, and he will reveal it to you. But it all starts with making better decisions in life for yourself. God is love and the sustainer of all existence—nothing else can measure up to him.

ABOUT THE AUTHOR

Anton Sears is a husband, father, mentor, and minister of God. Before becoming an author, Anton attended Liberty University Online in 2016 and achieved his Christian Ministry Certificate. Anton teaches the Holy Bible at his home along with his friends and family, and he runs his own youth group called Christ Over Everything. He along with other youth members go around the city of Cleveland and spread the gospel of Jesus Christ and perform random acts of kindness. Occasionally, he teaches at various churches also. Anton is a positive role model who loves adolescents and aspires to do nothing more than share the word of God with others and bring Jesus Christ into the lives of those oblivious of his greatness. For more information, email christovereverything1984@yahoo.com.

ANTON C. SEARS

SOURCES

G, Laurie. (1999). New Believer's Guide to How to Share Your Faith (Wheaton, IL: Tyndall House), 45.

McDowell, J. & McDowell, S. (2012). 77 FAQs About God And The Bible (Eugene, Oregon: Harvest House), 51.

Chapter 1

Manning, B. (2015). Abba`s Child: The Cry of the Heart for Intimate Belonging (Colorado Springs,Co: Tyndall House), 33.

Ortberg, J. (2014). Soul Keeping: Caring for The Most Important Part of You (Grand Rapids, Michigan: Zondervan), 103.

ANTON C. SEARS

www.ingramcontent.com/pod-product-compliance
Lightning Source LLC
Chambersburg PA
CBHW020516030426
42337CB00011B/415